Ocean Poetry Anthology 2025

Edited by A.M. Larks

Illustrated by Leslie Gonzalez

ISBN-13: 978-1-964880-04-4

Cover design and Illustrations: Leslie Gonzalez

Library of Congress Control Number:

Printed in the United State of America

TABLE OF CONTENTS

I.

II.

III.

Editor's Note

Organizing anything is always a taxing but rewarding task for me. Anthologies epitomize this concept. There are so many great poems, so many options of arrangement, so many theories to consider, so many opinions from so many people.

For me, I let the poems group themselves. There is always something that binds a poem to its buddy, like friends. Maybe it's a shared outlook or quality. Maybe it's how they play off one another and expand both. Maybe it's a shared tone or form of expression. Inevitably, those pairs begin to group and then those groups of pairs form a movement.

The first movement in this anthology captures a wider perspective. The poems look at the ocean stepped back from personal experience. In order to receive this mind-opening perspective, we must first "Listen" to the earth, to the ocean, to each other, to ourselves. This is why I have chosen the shortest poem in the anthology to open it. It is imperative for the journey ahead. It is only after we listen can we hear the song, the rhythm, the rhyme of those words uttered after. Only after listening can we hear how interconnected we all are on this planet, and as innovatively described in "Declaration of Interdependence".

Nothing so showcases our interconnectedness than the poems in the second movement where we, ironically, move into the personal. Our individual interactions with the ocean and its creatures unleash a myriad of feelings: joy, grief, anxiety in each of us. Each interaction is personal, fleeting, and yet, universal and timeless. These poems do not stand alone; they represent a larger conversation of humans and nature. They are in conversation with each other, depicting the range of human emotion elicited by our contact with nature, but also they are in conversation with the other poems in this anthology. They are all connected by this common thread. By writing, by nature, by reflection, by the ocean.

For the third movement, we return back to the wider perspective, with a renewed vision of our place in the world. We are individual but part of a whole. This section provides us a moment to reflect on how our personal use has damaged the wider ecosystem. It is this third section that has struck me in creating this year's anthology. So, many of us are observing human behavior and we are angry. We are interconnected to this planet and yet we act as if we do not need it, need to care for, can do whatever we want to it.

To me this third movement is what sets this year's anthology apart from its sibling, the inaugural firstborn child, the 2024 Ocean Poetry Anthology. I felt that tome was mostly a celebration of our love for the ocean, while, yes, recognizing the need for improvement. 2025 is speaking out loud, in the loudest possible way, with all the angst and disdain (very youngest child energy). The poems here are poignant, beautiful, and absolutely devasting. That so many authors in 2025 should feel this way points to a swelling, a rising taking place. Change is on the horizon.

Cue the "Rocky" theme song.

This is our small contribution to the cause. We hope that by reading all of these author's works, you too will be so moved to tackle a different future this year and in all the days ahead.

I.

Listen

By Amanda Niamh Dawson

In so subtle a swell
A shell

Siren of the Baltic Sea
By Gerard Thompson

As a storm settles, a whispering breeze,
he hears the songs of the Baltic Sea.
A forsaken traveler, lost and worn,
his shadow stretched from lives once torn.

The storm that raged now calms the sky,
but in its wake, the past won't die.
Memories cling like salt in air,
the ghosts of old wounds that still despair.
His heart, a shipwreck, crumbles within,
a sail that tore, but couldn't win.

Then her voice, a whispering breeze,
promises a fate both sweet and deceased.
He feels the pull, the dark desire,
her gaze ignites a dangerous fire.
Her beauty is a trap, a silent plea,
a dance for the dead beneath the sea.

But in her heart, she feels the sting,
a tender ache that makes her sing.
For the first time, her soul is torn,
for him, a love she never mourned.
Gintaré, bound by fate's cruel thread,
now wishes to spare him the dead.
Her voice, so soft, is filled with grief,
a siren's curse, beyond belief.

She sees the traveler, tired and lost,
but she, too, bears the heavy cost.
Her eyes weep for him, but she knows,
her heart is shackled by the undertow.
To love him means to break her bond,
but her curse is something she can't respond.

To take him in her arms, to set him free—
would unravel the darkness of the sea.

Drawn to her voice, so soft and sweet,
he falls beneath her rhythmic beat.
Gintaré, a name he's never known,
but in her eyes, the abyss is shown.
A weary heart, seeking release,
she promises an end, a fleeting peace.
Her song, a hook in his fragile soul,
a tempting lie, but makes him whole.

Her skin, like moonlight, pale and cold,
her secrets hidden, stories untold.
Her eyes leam, a stormy shore,
a siren's kiss, an open door.
In her embrace, he's lost, undone,
forever claimed by the waves and sun.
Her song—no mercy, no regret—
draws him closer, his past reset.

A traveler, bound by what he's left,
haunted by the lives he's never kept.
He stumbles deeper into her trance,
a victim of fate, not choice, not chance.
Her song, a hook in his fragile skin,
pulling him closer to the abyss within.

Beneath the waves, where no man should be,
his body drifts, as his soul is free.
A mind forgotten, a love decayed,
forever bound where the siren's played.
In the depths of the abyss, where none should be,
his soul remains with the Siren of the Baltic Sea

Orpheus as Waves of the Nazaré Canyon
By Anastasios Mihalopoulos

He thrums his dumb grief-infused surges into the bedrock
Tries to carve something out of something already carved out

already so hollow, that to press further, is to tear through
like a clumsy potter's hands on a wheel of clay.

The next wave comes, and then the next.
Thunderous clatter on thunderous clatter.

His grief, a song that doesn't know how to end
keeps playing its pre-Cambrian meter

loud and cantankerous as the tectonic rumbling
of the seafloor, pounding its way with want to break through

to some Eurydice beneath the sea. That isn't there,
That doesn't hear his music because it will never

have an audience that listens for more than a barre
or two. Species will arrive then go extinct

before they develop the proper ears for this melody
like the flash of lightning that dances ahead of the thunder

this erosive need, these heavy lyrical vibrations
in place of sentences, of letters. The voice of a wave,

energy-contained, crashes, and releases his song
of saturated sea-swell to split the canyon open.

And yet, somehow, the music weaves itself in,
His verses braid itself with the winter storms

which get buried in the rock of the earth that reverberates
and waits until one of us, lazily places an ear to the dirt and listens.

The Overfull Universe

By Katy E Ellis

In time the Earth cracks apart
and barnacles leak in

spread across the cement breakwater

up and down steps that lead to sand.

They leave circles everywhere after
their deaths—like white lipstick kisses
on whale-wide granite stones.

For years my skin has been pulling tidelands
from my heart, which balloons enough
to hold them.

Occasionally I find starfish in my hands—

every spring their stench feeds gardens

—I almost wrote *gargoyle* but their faces
ward off no evil.

All my losses are equally meek
but valid: green trustworthy machinery
to ride across the sea.

I will cull the worst weeds

I will, today, make myself
hear the sound of capillary waves
and glory in our similarities:
my blood a saltmarsh

my tongue the feather
catching magnified suns.

Shadows of the Sea
By Joseph Tetro

To step into the sleep
of the shore
the sea turning far
from itself

its gray green eyes fading
across the world.

What can we remember
here without light
to recall the day

the morning hidden
from our hands
behind the doors
we did not open.

In every sky
the night closes
its cup of stars

and all the maps
that ever were
cannot free us
from our secrets

the life we saw
when there was nothing to see.

Marine
By DH Jenkins

Sunrise—and the shock of white hot light
turns the sky yellow,
mustard at the edges, lemon in the air,
incandescent at its center near
the sun, like a citronella candle.

Over the isthmus, sails flow red w/dawn
headed for Majorca,
seagulls crying in the distance.

The green hills seem to crouch beside
the boats, which are slicing thru waves,
tilting against sky.

At the sea's surface, a floating purple mass
of weed, octopus, and other flotsam
and sundry jetsam.

But near to us are the blue depths not yet
penetrated by the piercing rays of sun—

Translucent blue, reviving an ancient,
mysterious mood asleep since our ancestors
navigated by the stars.

Layers of blue which when glimpsed
in this light take us back to a calmness
of certainty & buoyancy;

The place where dreams come from,
slowly rising, in waves to be remembered—
albeit momentarily—then dissipating
to micro sediment cast into the salt-sun air.

A Painterly Storm
By Pamela Moore Dionne

Dark tourmaline
waves deepen,
shattered by the scrape and scratch
of a stiff-brushed wedge,
angled with cadmium red
and ochre for accent,
forcing the eye
to a rocky shore
where white caps
are pallet-knifed
onto the cusp
of a gale-tossed
sea, in a bay
without safe harbor.
There is a veil of watered air
– falling falling –
vertical fan strokes,
long, lightly applied.
We see through
to a vague landscape
where everything is sodden,
tinted hopelessly gray.
Where the day feels like weight
and weight wears weary hours
down to bone – as though
applications of color
have been scraped away
by a restless artist – distraught
by what is wrought.

Declaration of Interdependence

By Aishatu Ado

WHEREAS: Water-bodies suffer breach-wounds under human reign,

AND WHEREAS: Blue-worlds: re-named from kin to commodity,

THEREFORE: These salt-truths bind all beings through water's covenant:

ARTICLE I

Claim no tides. Own no currents. Possess no waves.
These blue rhythms—ancient before speech,
cradle conquest and communion,
delivering home or drowning deep—
ocean-memory outlasts all flags.

ARTICLE II

Breath-right: inviolable.
Plankton-born oxygen spirals—
water-to-air-to-lung-to-blood.
Ocean kinship, severed, unmakes all.

ARTICLE III

Plastic-freedom: non-negotiable,
as polymer-fragments migrate through:
—gill-filter
—gut-wall
—placental-gate
—fetal-brain
—mother's milk

Ocean: unwilling vessel of mortal forever-trash.

ARTICLE IV

Dissolve all map-fictions:
territorial waters, sovereign seas, ownership-lines—
empire's parchment-boundaries
meaningless to water's unbound truth.
Salt knows no borders.

AMENDMENT I

Blood remembers: exact salt-percentage
of first-ocean birthwaters.
Cells recall: swimming before walking.
Tears match: precise chemistry of origins.
Bodies never forget their blue beginning.

AMENDMENT II

For Atlantic-sleep-graves: reparations.
For stolen harbors: restitution.
For emptied nets: justice.
For silenced shore-songs: remembrance.
The ledger of waves forgets nothing.

II.

Hug the Earth
By Christiane Hinterman

I carved a coast
inside my chest

and my breath
was a wave

      way out

where the land
slipped off the edge

      a whale
      came up for air

      and my heart
      became a boat

            happy and lost

      trusting that the ocean
      would always

hug the earth.

A Holiday in Hua Hin

By Frank William Finney

We rode horses
on the beach
that year:

our hands
on the reins
before the rains

would slip
the sea slugs
back into shells.

How lucky
we were
she didn't fall—

My daughter,
so young
and at a gallop

rode like a centaur
Too close to towels
and their herd

of frail riders
looking terrified
beside the tide.

How grateful I felt
for the peace
that followed:

the tracks
of our four feet
intact

leaving trails
of gratitude
in the smooth, white sand.

Maui Check-in Bag

By Carmen Jackie

In my hardshell suitcase I packed my hibiscus print cover up,

embroidered Mexican blouse,

straw sun hat that I paid way too much for,

booty shorts with a bit of lace,

glittery eyeshadows,

pearl kissed lip-gloss,

macrame tote filled with beach reads,

wedge espadrilles for when I want to look taller,

and the two-piece bathing suit that I am finally going to wear...I promise.

things to remember next time you are on a boat
By Kerry J Heckman

1. wear a jacket—it's always colder than you think
2. stand near the front but to the side where the wind isn't as intense
3. hair in a braid or wear a hat (or else come home with a tangled mess)
4. the proper boat beverage is hot chocolate
5. dramamine for choppy waters—patches behind ears don't work
6. hold on to the railing when picking up speed
7. if you can reach it—pull trash from the water
8. fast approaches lead to bumpy landings
9. despite the swells vessels are built to be seaworthy
10. a whale spout looks like a geyser rising from the waves
11. keep a thousand yards between the boat and endangered orcas
12. even if you can't see it—there is always another shore
13. find joy in the rugged mystical headlands
14. don't stay away from the ocean for too long
15. say thank you thank you thank you to the tides
16. never underestimate the power of water—to destroy or heal
17. wish on bioluminescence the same as shooting stars
18. every body of water is in the blue eye of a wild horse
19. to be drawn out from the edge is to begin again
20. this might be the closest you get to metamorphosis

Brief Encounter

By Ruth Mota

At first, they elude me
slithers of silver light
in this balmy Brazilian bay.

Trapped in my puffy vest
I stay afloat but cannot follow.
My legs dangle as the dolphins
dip and crest and dive away.

But what's this
squeaking?
Thick pink tongue and rows of little
tooth-saws quiver in my face.

She turns, floats belly up beside me.
I pass my hand along her taut skin.
There's new life bulging here.

Then the others come
encircle me and
offer up their bellies too.

O that I had more hands!
O that I could hold
this much joy!

Rincon Overtures

By Mike Sluchinski

at rincon you hear it
if you can get to the beach and
for inlanders the first thing
is the waves and you hear the sound
coming in and curling curving
around the point and who could it
be there must be something going
on out there and drifting the waves
come in and drive around the point
hitting the shore and some are
out there surfing the fan the
spread if you look from above
rincon heartbeat waves pumping
there's this one motion something
living that we don't control and
the waves keep coming and no
one can stop them their mind
their own and we do nothing
do nothing but play there rincon
an old 57 chevy and some longboards
and shortboards some paddling out
no one smells coffee till the
thermos opens and the sun
has just come up and there's
light offshore winds dawn patrol
swoons and when it's good like
that day you know the kind
warm already and the waves
pressed out of the ocean's
machine out there in the depths
soft overtures to the sun and water
notes undone that come again and again
the surfers don't need to talk and don't
the music plays as it always had
because there's only

one thing left to do after
avoiding the others just
get out there paddle out
and surf

One Must Have a Mind for Summer

By The Poet Mj

bald sun
cloudless scalp
scatter brain heat

stir the vitamiser waves, with fins
and wear a sarong made of sand

middle hopes large,
youth thin
comb the mind for whales that float

salty zephyrs, with
seaweed filled nostrils

long dreams, the
cone, horizontal skies in
ice cream moons

this is our times
thrust surf in sexualities
behind the rocks crash, and

one loud, last applause, for the sun
squeezing in the hours

Under the Waves

By Liz DeGregorio

Lying still on the beach, grains of sand billowing over my sun-warmed body,
I thought: I'll never know such happiness again.

The waves didn't crash that day – they rocked back and forth,
grabbing the shoreline, then releasing it,
a peaceful rhythm that put me in mind of
      a baby in the womb, nestled in tight,
      in their warm wet world.

My mind bakes a bit in the sun; my concerns dissolve like
      so much sea foam,
my muscles loosen as I feel myself melting into the blanket,
      and the hot sand underneath.

To be alone with sensation is a gift –
your breath in sync with the ocean's salt, the wind and the passage of
      white clouds above.

I dip under the waves again and again.

How to Accept Gifts from the Sea

By Sarah Lacker Vogel

The sea gives gifts
as the universe grants wishes:
at random, in subtle ways-
easily overlooked.

Perch yourself at the edge of the world,
but keep moving
so the vastness of the sea
doesn't swallow you whole.
Wipe the sun from your eyes,
look at everything.

Even a fragment
can be a work of art.
What once was home or shield
or body of a living thing,
now turned and smoothed
by salt and time.
Are you worthy of such a gift?

When one finds your gaze,
do not look away.
The ocean will try
to dissuade you-
knocking your legs with waves,
salt coating your sun-baked body.
to finally rediscover awe.

Walk steadily against the
thought that you are weak and small.
Plunge your hand into
the cold water,
and acknowledge the hidden lives
that surround you.

The shell is solid
against unsteady sands.
Is it not the one you sought?
With perfect whorls and even color?

Perhaps it's the one you need.
With irregular patterns,
splintered with cracks and holes-
lift it to your ear.
Listen to the universe it contains.

After all, why would the sea so willingly
give up such a gift?
For a child to dig up and discard?
For the artist to paint with plastic?
Or for the wanderer lost on the shore,
hearing the way their own heartbeat
blends with the pulse of the sea,

Ojo de agua
Celestun, Merida, Yucatan

By Miriam Calleja

Como se dice?
The eye of the water flows easy as an epiphany as the boat rocks.
Sweet water rises but quickly mixes with salt water and soon they become
indistinguishable, as though the sweetness never happened.

                                        And is that why
                                   they tell you it is better
                                   to have loved and lost?

Como se dice? There is nothing to say about the silence of water flowing
how I reach for your hand when my eyes see beauty.
The eye of the water sees sweetness and saltiness mix
and it never blinks.

still waters

By Juliette Zhu

I.   church bells and runoff

i was never baptized, but i like to think that storms on friday evening
can wipe me cleaner than jesus ever could, before i knew that
pew time meant the swallowing of droplets unshed
as unbelievers we stood in a desert of fish hooks on jawbones
yet could never ask why our altar of sins bled bright red.

II.   a drowning at the kissing grove

saturday mornings turned us into bog bodies
facing an early embalming, a citrine storm enough to bring us
to our knees, no, we never knelt for anything but a game of hide and seek
with nowhere left to run, i found a hiding spot
at the bottom of the lake, just upshore
just above the run off, just in front of the overwatered grove
where you sunk heaven to me.

III.   the baptism

sundays were as clear as the days before the flood
but you knew that in mud puddles, our emulsion
sits still in decay

You're too clean. Give me back my lost time. I tasted my grandma's candy for the first time in nine years, let me tell you about it. Can you give me just a little bit of grace?

Water baby, cry baby
For Anthony P. Manieri

By Themo H Peel

My uncle called me "fat boy".
And the more I cried and screamed
and shared my hurt the more he laughed.
Stolen slices of ham were the simplest solace
when nothing felt safe besides
an aching stomach sick with regret.

So, I wore t-shirts in pools,
the sticky second skin a thin
veneer declaring every curve of shame.

Boys told me I wasn't a twink or bear –
too heavy hearted and stretch mark
scarred to be of use in bed or bars.
I ran heels to rags at rugby
and they laughed at how my shorts rode
up the middle because thick thighs provided
warning signs of the grotesque body beneath.

So, I ate olives in public and
laxative soaked sponges in the dark,
segmented abs showing all my unhappy parts.

I stand on a beach
with a crowd of men, laughing.
I wear nothing but speedos and together
we careen over rocks and waves
moving through muck and sand –
boobs, bellies, thighs jiggling,
stinging surf bouncing
off glistening bodies, bare.

So, I scream, I stomp, I share

away the fear that I am not enough.

I show off my life and lines.
I cry with pride for the world in me -
this beautiful body of mine.

Dina's Disappearance
By Virginia LeBaron

Kiawah, 1981, dusk

waves unfurl

onto the shore

like ribbons

of black velvet

we shed our clothes

in the salt-bittered breeze

race into a blistered sea

The Hospital, 1991, dinner

It frightens me

how you refuse to eat

scapulae pushing like plates

against your sallow skin

I want you to rise

like the tide sliding

under your ribs

gentle as a butter knife

cast aside the dark

    silhouettes drawn-in tight

surrounding our heads like shrouds

Solitary Car

By Tamara MC

I am the only one alone on this train,
watching families cluster, friends laugh.
Mile Post Seventy-Two slides past the window,
avalanche protection standing guard.

Morning haze from last night's forest fire
scents the air like distant campfires.
I missed the bus downtown yesterday—
another small journey undertaken alone.

It seems like old times:
everyone else, and me.

Not lonely, not ecstatic,
just present in the space between.

The inland arms of Alaska stretch
like reaching hands I cannot grasp.
Turnagain's tides rise forty feet,
surfers in dry suits riding the tsunami.

Two thousand moose roam unseen,
inhabiting the vast wilderness.
Are they ever lonely, I wonder,
or simply content in solitude?

Those with family and friends seem happier—
or do they simply seem so from a distance?

Green and green and white
and grey and grey and brown.
The colors blur together
as the train moves forward,
carrying me alone.

Kai Hānau o ka Pō

By Keri Ka'iulani Picolla

Not born of the sands of my ancestors,
  my piko, discarded beneath humming fluorescent lights,
  lost to the whispers of pōhaku.

My iwi displaced,
  my mother's iwi displaced—
  her hope, when she finally returned to Pō,
  was that Moananuiākea—
  vast, knowing, endless—
  would carry her home.

Her feet pressed upon the sands of her beginning,
  her birth, her first breath,
  like her kupuna before her.

The ache she must have felt—
  to have been uprooted,
  to birth her own babies
  onto faraway sands.

Yet Moananuiākea knows me,
  like it knew her.

I was born of Pō,
  of kai,
  of her.

Carried by my mother,
  and her mother before her—
  generations held in creation's waters,
  nested in the wombs of those who came before.

If the sands could not care for me,

then I was a child meant for the waters.

Let the waters speak my name,
  let them remember her,
  remember me,
 those who came before,
  and those who come after.

Weaving my name into theirs,
  into the tides,
  to the moon.

They named me,
like they named my daughters—
and though we were not born of the sands,
we are born of the waters of Pō.

III.

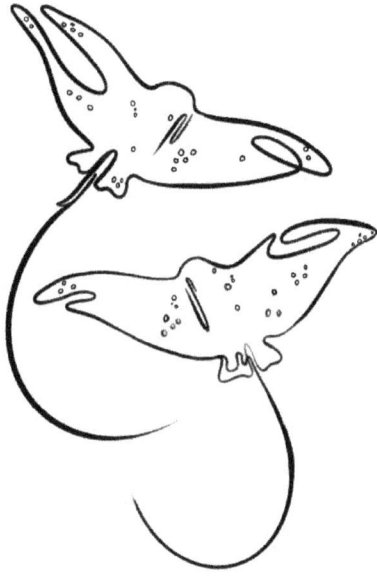

Pacific

By Jonathan Memmert

perfect form *waves* roll ashore perfect form
footprints litter beach sands
imperfect beings on imperfect grounds
leave little trace

submerge rush waters
splash remembrance
tides reconnect
from krill to whales
to undulating schools of flashing fishes
untraceable by land bound eyes

off coast earthquakes shear coastlines
sea level rise bathes emotions
behold oceania species in plastics be-held
depth dive dimensions

invisible liquid
washes my focus out of focus
wet conveniences nature both sides
stir duets in immersion
shows me ways never thought lived
disappeared on bleached out reefs

Click Here for the Latest Biotoxins

By Vivian Faith Prescott

Update: Notes of caution,
your own risk—long after the algae bloom

kids at culture camps, walkers at Starrigavan North,
fish at Gartina Creek, swimmers at Nahku Beach,
kayakers and canoers at Shaman Point, Amalga Harbor

air temp, salinity, water temp, phytoplankton,
biotoxins monitored

curve of shoreline, starred map,
satellite zoomed in—how are we seen and unseen—
advisory for all species—please
pay attention
please pay attention

blue mussel, butter clam, little neck, cockle, and horse

The light from the sun moves through ocean
whiplike hairs, divides and divides
blooms like flowers

The Whales Are Filling Up

By Diana Woodcock

The whales are filling up
on plastic shards, no fault
of their own, dying from starvation
once bellies lack room for fish.
How I wish it wasn't true.

How I wish we could light a match
to the Great Pacific Garbage Patch,
and destroy it once and for all.
The glaciers and ice sheets are melting,
the seas rising, spilling their salt

onto farmers' coastal crops, killing
them. How do we stem the tide?
How do we undo the damage
and right the wrongs? The whales
no longer can hear their own songs

because of all the underwater drilling
and fracking. Half the world's
now charred and smoke-choked,
the other half flooded and drowning
in debris. Woe are we.

But here's what will save me
from despair this one day:
the sight of one Great Blue heron
soaring over the river,
the sound of one Wood thrush,

a chorus of crickets at dusk. I do not
ask for much—only that my senses
might remain sharp, my hopes and
dreams continue to rise up with
the meadow lark to the skies.

ABC News Reports: Orca Mother Carrying Her Dead Calf Again

By Madelyn Meyers

Again, the reporter intones,
Again, this curious behavior.
A small body pink where white should be,
Too limp and yet she gently noses him up from
Water pitted with plastic.

7 days now she carries him
And she remembers—
7 years ago, when another son was carried
Bloated, pink:
1000 miles, 17 days.
And she wonders—
What distances covered could ever quantify her grief?

Does she understand? —the reporter asks—
But, oh,
She knows that
Grief is a language
And those who pretend to rules of convention
Misunderstand the point of her rites.

And when she rips rudders off ships
And when they ram their soft bodies into hard hulls
She knows we are to blame.

It turns out
This curious behavior
Is not so curious in the end.

Note: *J-35 is a female killer whale who was spotted by researchers in the beginning of January 2025, in Washington's Puget Sound, carrying the lifeless body of her calf on her nose. Seven years ago, she had lost another calf and performed this same rite. Scientists note that 50% of killer whale calves die before their first birthdays and that human overfishing and pollution are the chief contributors endangering this species. Perhaps, when we read of killer whale pods ramming into ships and sinking them, we should not be so surprised by their anger.*

Rogue Whales

By Kathleen Holliday

We be the podless ones.
The lost ones.
Don't wanna be found.

We fin, we slice the scene.
Those Great White?
Give over to the Black & White.
Give us sea room.

We be posses of two or three,
cruise those Isles
of the Rising Sun.
We be ronin.

We ram & sink those boats.
Rattle some cages.
We run the Middle Sea.

We chase Big Blues.
Their littles we run down,
savage & drown.
Because we can.

We be the podless ones.
The lawless ones.
Killers of the Sea.

Vengeance is the Sea
By Richard Stimac

Like a sea monster risen from the depth,
a hulking beast of trash twists against itself.
Ground infinitudes insinuate in our food,
our drink, our breath. We become what we discard.

Entropy exists in chartered corporate waters
while governments map plans for remediations.
We are at the end of history. The future is cancelled.
There is no end but the endless repetition of today.

I am haunted by a vision of the sea
that once covered all the earth.
Retreating with the waters was the Goddess
of Vengeance: Furies, Kali, Leigong.

Once cathedrals rose to Mary, minarets to Allah,
stupas to Buddha, ziggurats to Ishtar.
Today, conglomerates rebrand, like chattel,
the faculties of human thought and freedom.

There is no revelation to be had.
Vengeance has come to rest.
She is a Leviathan beached
upon a desolate strip of sand

to labor with divine birth pangs.
But the Messiah is stillborn.
Like a salty tide forever rising,
this Maria pursues bitter retribution.

I see it, in satellite photographs,
more clearly in my soul, this transgressing
sea as it slowly devours the coasts.
It is not dust but the sea to which we return.

Cast Away
By Michele M Miller

here i am
desperate muscle
clawing at bones in dunes
shying from sorrow chilled by foam
the isle is
then isn't
then is out of reach
drags me deep in its wake
disappears when i strain
to hear the sirens
unintelligible
intentionally
they make me lean
deceived to the edge
riddle my husk of boat
with thirst

for butter
smelling of farmhouse
wet grass fertile earth
the breath of the white calf
fresh from nursing
my mouth bawls
tongues of sand suckle me
starve on my fingers
my knees my sacrum my feet

i am betrothed
to salt and kelp
alive
in the hand mirror of this moon
i try to float in
what is given to me i wear
in pockets of my skin
tomorrow i'll return
my name with the point of a finger
to haunt the shore
i'll drink all the way down

to the seed at the snail's beginning
hear birth in every whorl
frantic to be held captive
a homeless crab
in a fist that fits

It is what it does to you on the inside
By Amanda Cruise

when the pelicans return
soundless in their hundreds
long ribbons of black silk
on raw canvas

brushstrokes that appear
and disappear
over pacific bluffs
urchin purple

at low tide
air water earth that smell
of kelp and heat and pollen
on shore pine

      it is what it does to you
      on the inside

this sky dancing prayer
benign incantation
of weightless grace
that says yes

please to wet
on thirsty skin yes please
to silver and salt for breakfast yes
please to a time   before

we plucked and sprayed and pushed
them to the brink

twice

first   by hunting them for hat feathers
then   by watching the still-feathered parents
          crush their eggs with their chicks
          still inside because

we

did not tell them that

we

      made their shells too thin because

we

failed to stop the ddt

~

and now
they are landing and collapsing
in backyards and parking lots emaciated
dehydrated lethargic cold and confused and

we   don't even seem
       to know
       why that is

what it does
to us on the inside
that makes it hard to resist
this urge

to disown
all of it resist
this urge to reach
for the next updraft

        and beg their forgiveness

say yes please to a time
before

when human meant we
knew how to tend and protect
the millions of prayers in our borrowed skies

benign incantations
of weightless grace

sky   dancing

        prayers

ABOUT THE AUTHORS

Aishatu Ado (she/her) is an Afro-German author, poet, and peace technologist, who advocates for social justice. She is the 2025 winner of the 68th Jerry Jazz Musician Short Fiction Award and a 2025 Clarion West fellow. Her work has earned support from fellowships with Tin House, VONA, Voodoonauts, Roots Words Wounds, and the Hurston/Wright Foundation. Aishatu weaves transformative Afro-feminist cosmovisions as both a visual and literary artist, drawing from ancestral oral traditions and mythologies. In Aishatu's poetic alchemy, reality bends to imagination's will, each word a spell cast in Africansurrealist ink. Her work is published or forthcoming in *Parables of AI in/from the Majority World Anthology*, the literary NFT collection *To Each Their Own Reality, Liminal Spaces*, and *Mythic Winter: A Science Fiction and Fantasy Anthology*. More at: aishatu.carrd.co

Miriam Calleja is an award-winning Pushcart-nominated poet, writer, workshop leader, and translator. Her work has appeared in *platform review, Odyssey, Taos Journal, plume, Modern Poetry in Translation, humana obscura*, and elsewhere. She has published full collections and chapbooks. Her latest chapbook is titled *Come Closer, I Don't Mind the Silence* (BottleCap Press, 2023). Miriam lives in Birmingham, Alabama. Read more on miriamcalleja.com.

Amanda Cruise (she/her) is a third culture kid who grew up in Rome and New York City with two religions, three passports, four languages, and a big, blended family. Her work includes photography, painting, printing, land art, poetry, and memoir. Her poetry has appeared in the *Noyo Review, The Bloom*, and soon to be published *Spirit of Place*: Mendocino County Women Poets Anthology. Her photography and other artwork have been exhibited in the US, Germany, Netherlands, Turkey and Thailand. Her creative path, like her life, continues to be non-linear and she likes it that way. She currently lives on a cliff above the Pacific in Mendocino on Northern Pomo land and loves to make stone balance sculptures by the ocean, eat homegrown artichokes, play her hand pan, talk to the plants in her garden and drink tea, exuberantly. www.amandacruise.com

Amanda Niamh Dawson lives in Sonoma County, California, 7 miles from the coast, no traffic lights. She writes about stars, oceans, and botany. She loves rap and rhymes. A poem won an award in the 2023 Poetry Society of Michigan's Peninsula Poets Contest and work has appeared recently in *Pomona Valley Review, Literary Yard, The Ulu Review*, and *Kelp Journal's The Wave*. Instagram: @thedawsonian

Liz DeGregorio (she/her) is a poet, writer and editor whose work has appeared in *Electric Lit, The Rumpus, Catapult Magazine, Lucky Jefferson, ANMLY, SCARS Magazine, BUST, Ghouls Magazine, OyeDrum Magazine, Blink Ink, Morbidly Beautiful, Dread Central,* and other publications. She's also performed at the award-winning storytelling series Stranger Stories.

Pamela Moore Dionne is a Port Townsend, Washington poet/writer/visual artist. She is the author of two chapbooks *Paradox and Illusion* and *Taut Caesuras* from Finishing Line Press. Dionne earned her MFA from Goddard College.

Katy E Ellis is the author of *Forty Bouts in the Wilderness*, which was first runner-up for the 2024 MoonPath Press Sally Albiso award. Her other books include the prose-poetry-novel *Home Water, Home Land* (Tolsun Books), and an award-winning chapbook *Night Watch* (Floating Bridge Press). Her work has most recently appeared in *Mom Egg Review* and *SWWIM*, and in and Canadian journal *PRISM International.* Learn more at: http://www.katyeellis.com/

Frank William Finney is a poet from Massachusetts. A recipient of The Letter Review Prize for Poetry, his poems have appeared in *Brussels Review, Fairfield Scribes, The Hemlock Journal, Kelp Journal, Penn Journal of Arts and Sciences (PJAS), The Paradox Magazine, Songs of Eretz Poetry Review,* and elsewhere. His chapbook *The Folding of the Wings* was published in 2022 by Finishing Line Press.

Kerry J Heckman (she/her/hers) is a psychotherapist and writer based in Seattle, Washington. She is currently pursuing her MFA in Creative Writing at the Rainier Writing Workshop at Pacific Lutheran University where she serves as the assistant editor/contributing writer at the program's journal *Soundings.* Her work has appeared in *Sonic Boom, Whiptail, and The Heron's Nest,* among other publications.

Christiane Hinterman grew up along the lakeshores of Michigan where time in nature nurtured her curiosities. With undergraduate and graduate degrees in environmental education, she pursued a life spent in the outdoors. Her nature inspired poetry, art, and songwriting are all vital means of communication and expression. When not writing or making music, she works with adults and children to make meaningful connections and personal transformations through yoga, education, art, and nature therapy. She now lives in the mountains and along the rivers of Montana with her supportive husband, two spirited daughters, and three magical cats.

Kathleen Holliday lives on an island in the Salish Sea. Her poems have appeared in *The Bellingham Review, The Blue Nib Literary Magazine, Cathexis Northwest Press, New Ohio Review, Nimrod International Journal, Poet Lore, Poetry Super Highway, SHARK REEF, The Write Launch,* and other journals. She is a graduate of Augsburg University, Minneapolis, MN. Her chapbooks, *Putting My Ash on the Line,* (2020), *Boatman, Pass By* (2023), and *A Cage in Search of a Bird* (2025) were published by Finishing Line Press.

Writer and Artist **Carmen Jackie** is originally from Mexico and received her MFA from the University of California, Riverside. Most of Carmen Jackie's published short stories are set in Southern California. When she is not in her studio writing or painting, she enjoys teaching college students how to paint and construct their own garments. To see more of her art follow her on Instagram: @mrs.carmen_jackie

DH Jenkins' poems have appeared in *Jerry Jazz Musician, Global South, Kelp Journal,* and *The Ekphrastic Review.* He lives in New Zealand where he enjoys hiking in the Southern Alps, as well as snorkeling in the Pacific Islands. His new book of poetry, *Patterns on the Wall,* is available on Amazon.com.

Virginia LeBaron is a nurse and a poet. She has published one chapbook (*Cardinal Marks,* Finishing Line Press, 2021) and her writing has been supported by a fellowship with the Virginia Center for the Creative Arts and through the Lighthouse Poetry Collective. She is an Associate Professor of Nursing at the University of Virginia and lives with her family in Charlottesville, Virginia.

Dr. Tamara MC, a mermaid-loving Cancerian, has published in 80+ outlets including *New York Times, HuffPost,* and *Newsweek.* Her forthcoming book *Poetry for English Language Learning: 130+ Exercises for Teaching Language, Culture, and Identity in the English Language Classroom* will be published by University of New Mexico Press in 2026. Dr. MC's work explores themes of displacement, identity, and cultural memory through poetry, creative nonfiction, and multimedia art. She has been awarded residencies at Bread Loaf, Ragdale, and Virginia Center for Creative Arts, and received an Arizona Commission on the Arts Research and Development Grant. Sign up for her mermazing mailing list at www.tamaramc.com and follow her @tamarmcphd.

Jonathan Memmert is a poet who lives in New York City. His poetry has been published in various poetry journals, He has an MFA in Creative Writing from The City College of New York, He is the associate editor for the online poetry journal for emerging poets, *The Marbled Sigh*. My poem is a reflection on my time body-surfing the Pacific Coast of the US.

Madelyn Meyers lives and works under the labels of educator, writer, and wonderer. Her writings center on humanity's relationship with the natural world. She has recently published poetry in Moonstone Arts Center and *Open: Journal of Arts & Letters*.

Anastasios Mihalopoulos is a Greek/Italian writer living in Fredericton, New Brunswick. He received his MFA in poetry from the Northeast Ohio M.F.A. program and his B.S. in both Chemistry and English from Allegheny College. The winner of the 2024 Prism Review Poetry prize, his work has appeared or is forthcoming in *Scientific American, Ninth Letter, Fairy Tale Review, Pithead Chapel*, and elsewhere. He is currently pursuing a Ph.D. in Creative Writing and Literature at the University of New Brunswick.

Michele M Miller holds an MFA in creative writing from the University of Arizona. Prizes awarded for her poetry include an Arizona Commission on the Arts fellowship, and her thesis manuscript, "The Cinderella Heart," was chosen runner-up for the National Poetry Series, and the Kore Press First Book Prize. Her chapbook *The Pocket Museum of Natural History* is forthcoming as part of the New Women's Voices Series with Finishing Line Press. Michele writes and photographs in her heartland, the Sonora desert of Tucson, Arizona.

Melinda Jane – The Poet Mj is the author of eight books and two spoken word CD's. With works published in thirteen anthologies books around the world and one hundred and thirty-three individual written pieces published by fifty publishers mainly in The United States of America. And has had a poem nominated for "Best of the Net" in 2019.

Ruth Mota currently lives by the Pacific Ocean in Santa Cruz, California. Previously she lived by the Atlantic Ocean off the coast of northeast Brazil. Many of the 60 poems she has published reflect her love for the sea.

Themo H Peel (he/him) is a disabled, Black, LGBTQ writer and illustrator based in Edinburgh. He has poetry published in *The Wave, Arlington Literary Journal, Dillydoun Review*, and *Beyond Queer Words*. He holds a BA in Fine Art from Yale and an MSc in Creative Writing from Edinburgh University.

Keri Ka'iulani Picolla is a writer, photographer, and hula dancer, born and raised in the diverse tapestry of California's diaspora. A 2023 NAPALI Fellow—a leadership program cultivating emerging Native Hawaiian and Pacific Islander leaders—she is passionate about fostering community arts and advocating for authentic representation of Native Hawaiians in media. Her work explores themes of identity, heritage, and diaspora. Her writing has previously appeared in *Kelp Journal*, and she is currently working on *Letters from a President*, a hybrid memoir chronicling the decade-long friendship between her mother and Indonesia's President Sukarno. She holds an MFA in Creative Writing from UC Riverside and lives in Los Angeles.

Vivian Faith Prescott was born and raised on the island of K̲aachx̲ana.áak'w, Wrangell Alaska, in the Alexander Archipelago. She lives off the forest and sea at her fishcamp on the land of the Shtax'heen Kwáan. She's a member of the Pacific Sámi Searvi and founding member of Community Roots, the first LGBTQIA+ group on the island. She currently mentors writers through two Alaskan writers' groups: Blue Canoe Writers and the Drumlin Poets. She's the author of several poetry books, a collection of short stories, and a foodoir.

Mike Sluchinski thankfully writes from where his wife paid the rent. Read him in *The Literary Review of Canada, In Parentheses, The Coachella Review, Inlandia, Welter, Poemeleon, Lit Shark, Proud To Be Vol. 13, The Ekphrastic Review, MMPP (Meow Meow Pow Pow), Kelp Journal & The Wave, 'the fib review', Eternal Haunted Summer, Syncopation Lit. Journal, South Florida Poetry Journal (SOFLOPOJO), Freefall*, and more coming!

Richard Stimac has published a poetry book *Bricolage* (Spartan Press), two poetry chapbooks, and one flash fiction chapbook. In his work, Richard explores time and memory through the landscape and humanscape of the St. Louis region.

Joseph Tetro was born in New York City, and lived and worked in Alaska for several years while receiving his MFA from the University of Alaska, Fairbanks. He is the author of *A New York Bestiary* and co-publishes Winter Light Books, which prepares and produces children's books based on folk tales from

Ukraine.

Gerard Thompson is a writer from Liverpool who finds inspiration in travel, photography, and the profound pull of human connection. His work explores fate, longing, and the unseen forces that guide us. Siren of the Baltic Sea is a tale of love and surrender, where myth and reality blur beneath the tides. The poem is inspired by a real-life connection of two people.

Sarah Lacker Vogel is a poet who also serves as an elementary special educator and a bookseller in the Lower Hudson Valley in New York. While still unpublished, her poetry often explores the little moments of joy in everyday life, everyday sensations, and responding to art she finds around her. When she isn't writing, she can be found reading a cozy fantasy novel, enjoying a cup of tea, or cloud gazing.

Diana Woodcock Diana Woodcock has authored seven poetry collections, most recently *Reverent Flora ~ The Arabian Desert's Botanical Bounty* (Shanti Arts, 2025), *Heaven Underfoot* (2022 Codhill Press Pauline Uchmanowicz Poetry Award), *Holy Sparks* (2020 Paraclete Press Poetry Award finalist), and *Facing Aridity* (2020 Prism Prize for Climate Literature finalist). A three-time Pushcart Prize nominee and Best of the Net nominee, she received the 2011 Vernice Quebodeaux Pathways Poetry Prize for Women for her debut collection, *Swaying on the Elephant's Shoulders*. Currently teaching at VCUarts Qatar, she holds a PhD in Creative Writing from Lancaster University, where she researched poetry's role in the search for an environmental ethic.

Juliette Zhu is student at UC Berkeley studying Cognitive Science. She is a nationally distinguished poet, having been named the first-place winner of the 59th Annual Nancy Thorp Poetry Contest, a winner in the Tadpole Press 100-Word Writing Contest, and an alumna of the Kenyon Review Young Writer's Workshop and Iowa Young Writer's Studio. Her poetry has been published in *Cargoes, The Nature of Our Times, Tadpole Press, Sixfold*, and more.

www.ingramcontent.com/pod-product-compliance
Lightning Source LLC
Chambersburg PA
CBHW070500050426
42449CB00012B/3059